Turtlesoft

Turtle Graphics for Applesoft

Robert W. Gallup

DOS 3.3 version by Robert W. Gallup

ProDOS version by John Brooks

Produced by:
Brian Wiser & Bill Martens

 Apple PugetSound Program Library Exchange

Turtlesoft: Turtle Graphics for Applesoft

Published in 1983, 2016 by Apple Pugetsound Program Library Exchange.
Redesigned and expanded in 2016 by Apple Pugetsound Program Library Exchange.

www.callapple.org

ISBN 978-1-365-51899-7

ACKNOWLEDGEMENTS

Turtlesoft manual published in 1983 Copyright © by Robert W. Gallup. *Turtlesoft* software for DOS 3.3 and ProDOS Copyright © 1983, 2016 by Robert W. Gallup.

We would like to thank Robert W. Gallup for loaning his original Turtlesoft source code disk and supporting this new update. All sample programs were created by Robert W. Gallup.

Special thanks to John Brooks for converting Turtlesoft to ProDOS in 2016.

PRODUCTION

Brian Wiser → Design, Editing, Production
Bill Martens → Screenshots, Production

DISCLAIMER

CONTENTS

1.   Introduction 1

2.   Hardware Requirements 1

3.   Programs on the Disk 1
3.1 Main Program 1
3.2 Demonstration Programs 2

4.   Overview of Turtlesoft Features 3

5.   Loading Turtlesoft 4
5.1 Running the Demonstration Programs 4
5.2 ProDOS Demonstration Programs 4

6.   Using Turtlesoft Primitives 5
6.1 Command Format 5
6.2 Command Placement 5
6.3 Abbreviations 6
6.4 Primitives Descriptions 6

7.   Creating Your Own Command Procedures 10

8.   Programming Examples 12
8.1 Drawing a House 12
8.2 Creating a New Command – TRIANGLE 12
8.3 Creating More Commands – SPIN.TRIANGLE 13
8.4 Using Variables – Drawing a Spiral 14
8.5 Recursion – Making a Forest 14
8.6 Using Two Screens 16

9.   Error Messages 17

10.   Technical Information 18
10.1   Loading Turtlesoft and Memory Usage 18
10.2   Resetting the "&" Vector 18
10.3   Zero Page Usage 18
10.4   Conflicts with BASIC 19
10.5   Conflicts with GPLE 20

11.   References 20

12.   Quick Command Reference 21

Appendix A – Demonstration Programs 22
      Circles 22
      Galaxy 23
      Grub 24
      Berserk Singing Turtle 25
      Sunburst Turtle 25
      Spiral Square 26
      Quick Confusion 27
      Instant Turtle 28
      Dynatrack 31
      Sierpinski 34
      Windows 36
      Polystop 37
      Snowflake 38
      Spiral 40
      Figure Eight 41

Turtlesoft

1. Introduction

Imagine you have a robot turtle. You might think that rather strange, but try to imagine it anyway. Imagine further that this "turtle" can move around the floor in response to commands you give it such as: FORWARD and BACK, which tells the turtle to move forward or backward a certain number of steps; and RIGHT and LEFT, which tells the turtle to turn, in place, a certain amount right or left. As the turtle moves, it leaves a trail you can see. By giving the turtle the right commands, you can have it draw any shape you want.

Voila! You have Turtle graphics.

Your computer screen is the floor and the turtle is a triangle visible on it.

As you experiment with trying to draw shapes using Turtle graphics you may find that thinking in "turtle talk" is much easier for many things than thinking in the "coordinate talk" of normal graphics.

2. Hardware Requirements

Turtlesoft for DOS 3.3 requires any Apple II computer with at least 48K of memory.

Turtlesoft for ProDOS requires any Apple II computer with at least 64K of memory. (Apple II and Apple II Plus must have a Language Card installed).

3. Programs on the Disk

3.1 Main Program

TURTLESOFT is the program which provides the turtle graphics used by the following demonstration programs.

3.2   Demonstration Programs

The following programs have been included on the Turtlesoft floppy disk images for the purpose of demonstrating the actual Turtlesoft functions.

The Turtlesoft disk images can be downloaded from the Apple Pugetsound Program Library Exchange website at: www.callapple.org

Program Listings for the sample programs are included in the Appendix A section of this manual:

CIRCLES
GALAXY
GRUB
BERSERK SINGING TURTLE
SUNBURST TURTLE
SPIRAL SQUARE
QUICK CONFUSION
INSTANT TURTLE
DYNATRACK
SIERPINSKI
WINDOWS
POLYSTOP
SNOWFLAKE
SPIRAL
FIGURE EIGHT

4. Overview of Turtlesoft Features

a. 25 instructions (primitives) for control of the turtle.

b. A sound routine used with Turtlesoft graphics.

c. Turtlesoft has the ability to use both HI-RES screens.

d. One of the most important features of Turtlesoft is that it allows you to create your own command names. You can use the commands you define the same way you use Turtlesoft primitives from immediate mode or deferred mode. You can use your commands in the definition of other commands making for a naturally "top-down" programming environment to facilitate clear program design.

e. Turtlesoft has descriptive error messages to facilitate easy program debugging.

f. Error messages can be processed using ONERR.

g. All commands are accessed through the ampersand, making them simple to use within your program.

5. Loading Turtlesoft

You can load Turtlesoft by booting the Turtlesoft diskette. When Turtlesoft is loaded, the "turtle" will appear in the middle of the screen.

Booting the Turtlesoft diskette will erase any BASIC program you have in memory. If you want to save your program you can use an alternate way to load Turtlesoft.

DOS 3.3
Insert the Turtlesoft diskette and type:

```
BRUN TURTLESOFT
```

ProDOS
Insert the Turtlesoft diskette and select:

```
TURTLESOFT
```

5.1   Running the Demonstration Programs

After the turtle appears on the screen type RUN followed by the name of the program you wish to view. (see Section 3 above)

Some of the programs have instructions and some others might require a little experimentation. To stop any of the programs you can press the RESET key (or CTRL-RESET).

These programs can be a good source for learning some of the abilities of Turtlesoft as well as some techniques for using it.

5.2   ProDOS Demonstration Programs

If you are using the Bitsy Bye program to select the sample programs on the disk, simply select the sample program you wish to run. Bitsy Bye will automatically load TURTLESOFT if it is not loaded yet and then execute the program selected.

6.   *Using Turtlesoft Primitives*

When Turtlesoft is loaded, 25 instructions are made available for you to use. The instructions control the turtle and the Turtle graphics screen. These instructions are called "Primitives."

6.1   Command Format

Each instruction has the following general format:

```
&"name"arguments
```

Each instruction has a name and must begin with an ampersand and a quote (&"). Some instructions require numbers or variables after the name (arguments). If arguments are required, they must be preceded by a quote.

You can put a quote after the name even if it doesn't require arguments and you may want to do so (see next section).

6.2   Command Placement

A Turtlesoft command can be used in a program anywhere a BASIC command can be used. The use of quotes in Turtlesoft commands makes them somewhat like PRINT commands in BASIC. If you have an odd number of quotes in a PRINT command anything after the last quote on the line will be "eaten up".

It is the same with Turtlesoft commands. Sometimes this could be desirable, but if you want to use more than one command per line you have to make sure that all the Turtlesoft commands in the line contain an even number of quotes. This is no problem for Turtlesoft primitives that use arguments since they all need a second quote after the name. Other Turtlesoft commands don't strictly require a quote after the name. For these you will have to remember to add a quote if you want to put multiple commands on a line.

6.3   Abbreviations

All of the Turtlesoft primitives may be abbreviated. For each primitive
description below you will see one name with some letters underlined.
That is the command name and the minimum number of letters you
must include in order for it to be recognized. For many primitives
there is a second, two letter, abbreviation listed below the main
command name. These are designed to match abbreviations used
in the LOGO language and make program and programmer transfer
between LOGO and Turtlesoft easier.

6.4   Primitives Descriptions

All of the following primitives can be used in immediate or deferred
mode. You can try them as you are reading by typing in the command
with no line number or you can include them in programs by using
line numbers just like you would for any BASIC command. In
these descriptions "n" refers to that includes numbers, variables, any
arithmetic or functions.

&"DRAW"   This primitive puts the computer into Turtle
                      graphics mode. It clears the screen and places
                      the turtle in the middle of the screen pointing
                      up. When you first load Turtlesoft it will
                      automatically be in DRAW mode.

&"NODRAW"   This primitive is the opposite of &"DRAW" and
&"ND"   takes the computer out of Turtle graphics mode.
                      TEXT will do the same thing.

&"FORWARD"n   This primitive moves the turtle forward.
&"FD"n   "n" stands for the number of "steps" to take.

&"BACK"n   This primitive is the opposite of &"FORWARD"
&"BK"n   and moves the turtle back. "n" stands for the
                      number of steps to take.

&"RIGHT"n   This primitive turns the turtle to the right. "n"
&"RT"n   stands for the number of degrees to turn.

6

&"LEFT"n &"LT"n	This primitive turns the turtle to the left. "n" stands for the number of degrees to turn.
&"HOME"	This primitive moves the turtle to the center of the screen pointing up (the same place it starts in when you use &"DRAW").
&"PENUP" &"PU"	This primitive causes the turtle to lift its pen so it won't leave a trail when it moves.
&"PENDOWN" &"PD"	This primitive is the opposite of &"PENUP" and causes the turtle to lower its pen so it will leave a trail.
&"PENCOLOR"n &"PC"n	This primitive sets the color of the "ink" in the turtles pen. "n" stands for the color and may be 0 to 7. Colors 0 and 4 are black and can't be seen on a black background.
CLEARSCREEN" &"CS	This primitive clears the screen to the current background color (see &"BACKGROUND" below). It doesn't change the location or direction of the turtle.
&"BACKGROUND"n &"BG"n	This primitive redraws the screen background color, "n" stands for the background color and may be 0 to 7. The colors are the same as for &"PENCOLOR". &"BACKGROUND" interacts with the pen color in a rather unusual way. If the background is black or white (0, 3, 4, or 7) any pencolor may be chosen and the turtle will draw in that color. If the background is not black or white then the pencolor may only be of the same "flavor". That means that for background colors 1 and 2 the pen color may only be 0 through 3; for background colors 5 and 6 the pencolor may only be 4 through 7. If you specify a pen color that is the wrong flavor for a background the pen color will automatically be changed to a valid one.

&"FULLSCREEN" &"FS"	This primitive sets full screen graphics mode.
&"SPLITSCREEN" &"SS"	This primitive sets split screen graphics mode (bottom 4 lines are text).
&"HIDETURTLE" &"HT"	This primitive makes the turtle shape disappear from the screen. You can still move and turn it and it will leave a track if the pen is down.
&"SHOWTURTLE" &"ST"	This is the opposite of the &"HIDETURTLE" and causes the turtle shape to re-appear on the screen.
&"MOVETO"x,y &"MT"x,y	This primitive moves the turtle directly to a specific spot on the screen (x,y). The center of the screen is 0,0. The limits are -139 to +139 for the first number (x-axis); and -95 to +95 for the second number (y-axis).
&"TURNTO"d &"TT"d	This primitive turns the turtle to a specific angle. "d" stands for the angle and must be positive. 90 degrees is facing up and 0 degrees is facing to the right. Any value for "d" greater than 360 will be taken as the modulas of 360.
&"?WHERE"x,y	This primitive sets two variables, one to the x-location and one to the y-location of the turtle. "x" and "y" stand for variables and must be Real Type variables.
&"?DIRECTION"d	This primitive sets a variable to the direction of the turtle. "d" stands for the variable and must be of Real Type. "d" will have a value from 0 to 359.999

&"?COLLISION"c   This primitive sets a variable "c" to indicate
                  whether the turtle collided with any dot on the
                  screen the last time it was drawn. "c" stands for
                  the variable and must be of Real Type. If "c" is
                  returned as 0 then there was no collision.

                  Some limitations are:
                  a. The background must be black.
                  b. If the turtle is hidden "c" will always be
                      returned as 0.
                  c. The pen must be up. In some cases it will
                      work with the pen down but sometimes the
                      turtle will collide with the line it is drawing.

                  The demonstration programs DYNATRACK and
                  GRUB use &"?COLLISION.

&"SING"p,d   This primitive tells the turtle to "sing". "p" stands
                  for the pitch of the note to sing (0 - 255) and "d"
                  stands for the duration of the note (0 - 65535). A
                  pitch of 0 is a rest and no sound is made.

&"PRINTOUT name" This primitive will list your program starting with
&"PO name"   the command definition for "name" (see Section 7
                  "Creating Your Own Command Procedures").

The following two instructions can be somewhat complicated to use.
See Section 8 "Programming Examples."

&"SHOWSCREEN"n   This primitive causes the computer to display either
                  the Page 1 or Page 2 graphics screen. "n" stand for
                  the page number. If "n" is odd then Page 1 will be
                  displayed (default). If "n" is even then Page 2 will
                  be displayed.

&"DRAWSCREEN"n   This primitive causes all turtle commands to act
                  on either graphics screen 1 or 2. If "n" is odd
                  then everything will work on graphics screen 1
                  (default). If "n" is even then everything will work
                  on screen 2.

7. Creating Your Own Command Procedures

A command procedure consists of two parts:

    a. definition header
    b. definition body

The definition header consists of one line that begins with the word "TO" and is followed by a quote and the name you wish to give the command. The name may contain any character except a quote, blank, or semicolon and may be up to 233 characters long (if you really want). Here are some examples of valid definition headers:

```
100  TO "SQUARE"
110  TO "POLY"
200  TO "READ.DATA.FILE"
999  TO "WRITE.PROMPT"
100  TO "BALLON.FACTORY"
```

NOTE: The name you give to a command must not be the same as any Turtlesoft primitive or abbreviation.

The definition body consists of a sub-program using BASIC commands, Turtlesoft primitives or commands you have defined.

When you use your new command, the computer searches your program for the definition header, If the header is found then the computer begins to follow the commands in the definition body. RETURN in the definition tells the computer the definition is finished. It is just like a GOSUB/RETURN only you don't have to worry about line numbers. Here's an example of a definition header followed by a definition body:

```
100  TO "SQUARE"
110  FOR I=1 TO 4
120  &"FORWARD"50
130  &"RIGHT"90
140  NEXT I
150  RETURN
```

If you were to enter this program then try to RUN it, it wouldn't work. That is because line 100 is not a valid BASIC command. The way to use a definition is to use the name the same way you would in using a Turtlesoft primitive. To use the SQUARE definition you would type:

```
&"SQUARE"
```

If you wanted to be able to RUN the program you could add lines:

```
10  &"SQUARE"
20  END
```

As mentioned before, this ability to create commands is very powerful. In the next section there are several examples showing the use of command definitions.

You can use the &"PRINTOUT name" primitive to easily list out the definition of a command. Try typing:

```
&"PRINTOUT SQUARE"
```

The listing should start with line 100 where the definition for SQUARE begins. Notice that you don't put a quote before the name SQUARE when using it in &"PRINTOUT name".

8. Programming Examples

8.1 Drawing a House

Here is a program that uses only Turtlesoft primitives to draw a house. Notice the &"DRAW" primitive at the beginning of the program to ensure that the computer is in draw mode when the program is run.

```
10   &"DRAW"
20   &"RIGHT"90
30   &"FORWARD"50
40   &"RIGHT"90
50   &"FORWARD"50
60   &"RIGHT"90
70   &"FORWARD"50
80   &"RIGHT"90
90   &"FORWARD"50
100  &"RIGHT"30
110  &"FORWARD"50
120  &"RIGHT"120
130  &"FORWARD"50
```

Some changes to try: Change the background color using the &"BACKGROUND" primitive. Try making the house larger or smaller. Add a door…

8.2 Creating a New Command – TRIANGLE

This program shows an example of defining a new command &"TRIANGLE". Note the use of the main program so you can RUN the program without getting a "SYNTAX ERROR" on line 110.

```
10   REM -- MAIN PROGRAM
20   &"DRAW"
30   &"TRIANGLE"
40   END
100  REM -- TRIANGLE DEFINITION
110  TO "TRIANGLE"
120  FOR S=1 TO 3
130  &"FD"50
140  &"RT"120
150  NEXT S
160  RETURN
```

12

Some changes to try: use &"BACK" rather than &"FORWARD" to draw the triangle. Change the triangle definition so that it isn't equilateral. Use &"LEFT" to define another command that draws a triangle to the left rather than the right.

8.3   Creating More Commands – SPIN.TRIANGLE

In this program, two commands are defined: &"TRIANGLE" and &"SPIN.TRIANGLE". &"SPIN.TRIANGLE" uses &"TRIANGLE" in its definition body.

```
10   REM -- MAIN PROGRAM
20   &"DRAW"
30   &"SPIN.TRIANGLE"
40   END
100   REM -- TRIANGLE DEFINITION
110   TO "TRIANGLE"
120   FOR S=1 TO 3
130   &"FD"50
140   &"RT"120
150   NEXT S
160   RETURN
200   REM -- SPIN.TRIANGLE DEFINITION
210   TO "SPIN.TRIANGLE"
220   FOR TN=1 TO 24
230   &"TRIANGLE"
240   &"RT"15
250   NEXT TN
260   RETURN
```

Changes to try: Change the number of degrees the turtle turns between each triangle. Make the program spin a shape other than a triangle.

8.4 Using Variables – Drawing a Spiral

This program uses a variable length to draw a spiral. Notice how a comment can be added to a definition header by placing it after a semicolon.

```
10   REM -- MAIN PROGRAM
20   &"DRAW"
30   &"BG"3
40   &"PENCOLOR"0
50   &"SPIRAL"
60   END

100   TO "SPIRAL":REM ** DRAW SPIRAL
110   SIDE=0
120   SIDE=SIDE+.5
130   &"STEP.AND.TURN"
140   GOTO 120

200   TO "STEP.AND.TURN":REM USES SIDE
210   &"FORWARD"SIDE
220   &"RIGHT"45
230   RETURN
```

Changes to try: make the spiral more or less dense by changing how the side changes with each "STEP.AND.TURN". Change the spiral by having a variable angle too.

8.5 Recursion – Making a Forest

This program uses the idea of recursion. Recursion is just when a command uses itself in its own definition. Recursion is a powerful way to solve some problems.

The three demo programs, GALAXY, SIERPINSKI, and SNOWFLAKE, all use recursion. Notice the use of random numbers. The POP in line 130 is used so the computer doesn't run out of memory by repeatedly calling FOREST without doing any RETURN's.

```
10   &"DRAW"
20   &"FOREST"
30   END

100  TO "FOREST":REM RECURSIVE COMMAND
110  &"PICK.SPOT"
120  &"DRAW.TREE"
130  POP:&"FOREST"

200  TO "PICK.SPOT"
210  X=RND(1)*200-100
220  Y=RND(1)*150-90
230  &"MOVE.TO.SPOT"
240  RETURN

300  TO "MOVE.TO.SPOT"
310  &"PENUP"
320  &"MOVETO"X,Y
330  &"PENDOWN"
340  &"TURNTO"90
350  RETURN

400  TO "DRAW.TREE"
410  &"PC"3
420  &"FD"10
430  &"LT"90
440  &"PC"1
450  &"FD"10
460  &"RT"120
470  &"FD"20
480  &"RT"120
490  &"FD"20
500  &"RT"120
510  &"FD"10
520  END
```

Changes to try: make the trees random colors. Make the trees random
sizes. Change the shape of the tree.

8.6 Using Two Screens

This is a trivial example of using the two Turtlesoft primitives:
&"SHOWSCREEN" and &"DRAWSCREEN".

```
10   &"DRAW"
20   &"PC"1
30   SIDE=100:&"DRAW.SQUARE"
40   &"SETUP.SCREEN.2"
50   &"PC"6
60   SIDE=110:&"DRAW.SQUARE"
70   &"HIDETURTLE"
80   &"FLIP.SCREENS"
90   END

100  TO "DRAW.SQUARE"
110  &"CENTER.SQUARE"
120  &"SQUARE"
130  RETURN

200  TO "CENTER.SQUARE":REM USES SIDE
210  &"PENUP"
220  &"MOVETO"-SIDE/2,-SIDE/2
230  &"PENDOWN"
240  RETURN

300  TO "SQUARE" ;USES SIDE
310  FOR S=1 TO 4
320  &"FD"SIDE
330  &"RT"90
340  NEXT S
350  RETURN

400  TO "SETUP,SCREEN.2"
410  &"HIDETURTLE"
420  &"DRAWSCREEN"2
430  &"CLEARSCREEN"
440  &"SHOWTURTLE"
450  RETURN
```

```
500  TO "FLIP.SCREENS"
510  FOR S=1 TO 100
520  &"SHOWSCREEN"2
530  &"SING"0,25 ;WAIT
540  &"SHOWSCREEN"1
550  &"SING"0,25
560  NEXT S
570  RETURN
```

9. Error Messages

There are 4 error messages Turtlesoft uses. They can be processed using ONERR. The messages, their error codes and what they mean are listed below.

TURTLE OFF SCREEN (code=17)
This means that a command tried to move the turtle out of the screen boundary.

NAME NOT FOUND (code=18)
This means that a name you used in a command primitive and a definition for it wasn't found program.

ANGLE NEGATIVE (code=19)
This occurs if you try to use &"TURNTO" with a negative angle as its argument.

WRONG VARIABLE TYPE (code=20)
This occurs if you use a variable that isn't of Real Type in the primitives: &"?WHERE", &"?DIRECTION" or &"?COLLISION". (see page 18 of your *Applesoft Reference Manual*)

Since Turtlesoft uses many Applesoft routines in its operation some standard BASIC errors may be generated, interpret them as you would in a BASIC command.

10. *Technical Information*

10.1 Loading Turtlesoft and Memory Usage

When Turtlesoft is loaded, it relocates itself underneath DOS starting at $9226 (37414) and rebuilds DOS's buffers below itself. If any other programs use this space they will interfere with Turtlesoft of vice-versa.

Turtlesoft normally loads at $4000 (16384) then relocates itself a described above. This may cause a problem if you load Turtlesoft from within a BASIC program when LOMEM has been set to between $4000 and $4B00 (19200). The load in that case would wipe out some or all of your BASIC program. To get around this you can use the "A$" parameter in the BRUN command to force Turtlesoft to do its initial run from any free memory.

There are two restrictions to running Turtlesoft anywhere in memory:

a. You can't have it run anywhere in the first Hi-Res graphics page.

b. Turtlesoft is about $B00 bytes long (2816 bytes or 11 pages) and you must have that much free room where ever you choose to run it.

10.2 Resetting the "&" Vector

If Turtlesoft stops working after you've loaded it, then it is possible that what's called the "&" (ampersand) vector has been wiped out. To reset the "&" vector you can do one of two things:

a. For Warm Start type CALL 37417. This will initialize just the "&" vector and will leave the turtle unaffected.

b. For Cold start type CALL 37414. This will initialize the whole Turtlesoft system as though it had just been loaded.

10.3 Zero Page Usage

The only use of Zero Page locations by Turtlesoft is for temporary storage. For these it uses locations normally reserved for Applesoft use. It does not use any of the free bytes normally saved for non-system use.

10.4 Conflicts with BASIC

Turtlesoft uses many of the Applesoft routines for drawing lines and doing floating-point calculations, etc. Because of this, there may be some conflicts with normal BASIC commands. Two cases where you use definitely will have some problems are:

a. If you use the BASIC Hi-Res instructions the turtle will forget where it is.

b. If you load or save any files from within a program the turtle will forget where it is.

If you want to do either of these, or anything else that interferes with the turtle you can use the two commands defined below to save the turtle's state before you interfere with it and restore it afterwards.

```
100   TO "SAVE.STATE"
110   &"?DIRECTION"TD
120   &"?WHERE"TX,TY
130   &"HIDETURTLE"
140   RETURN

200   TO "RESTORE.STATE"
210   &"PENUP"
220   &"MOVETO"TX,TY
230   &"TURNTO"TD
240   &"PENDOWN"
250   &"SHOWSCREEN"1
260   &"SHOWTURTLE"
270   RETURN
```

The &"HIDETURTLE" and &"SHOWTURTLE" primitives are used in these commands to ensure that the turtle "remembers" whether or not it is "visible".

These routines are used in the demonstration program INSTANT TURTLE to allow the saving and reading of pictures.

10.5 Conflicts with GPLE

If you don't have a Language Card then GPLE and Turtlesoft are incompatible since they both use the same memory. If you do have a Language Card then you can use GPLE because it will locate in the card.

There are some complications, though, depending on which system you load first. If you load Turtlesoft first then after you load GPLE you must type CALL 37417 to reset the "&" vector (see above). If you load GPLE first then you must use the "BRUN" method for loading Turtlesoft. In either case the "&" will not reconnect GPLE after a PR# or IN#. For this you must use CALL 1013 or CALL 1016 (described in the GPLE manual).

11. References

For a more complete description of Turtlesoft graphics and Turtle geometry, see the references below:

a. Abelson, H., diSessa, A. A. (1980), "Turtle Geometry: The Computer as a Medium for Exploring Mathematics", MIT Press.

This book is designed for teaching high school or college geometry but the first couple of chapters have a very good introduction to Turtle graphics.

b. Papert, S. (1980), "Mindstorms: Children, Computers and Powerful Ideas." New York: Basic Books.

This is an excellent book covering concepts behind the development of LOGO, a computer language that is famous for its use of Turtle graphics. It is very readable and presents good explanation of how Turtle graphics can be a useful tool to help people think and learn.

12. Quick Command Reference

The following command chart shows all of the Turtlesoft commands
and their functions in a quick, easy to use reference format.

Command	Alternate	Action
&"DRAW"		Sets DRAW mode.
&"NODRAW"	&"ND"	Sets NODRAW or TEXT mode.
&"FORWARD"n	&"FD"n	Moves turtle forward 'n' steps.
&"BACK"n	&"BK"n	Moves turtle back 'n' steps.
&"RIGHT"n	&"RT"n	Turns the turtle right 'n' degrees.
&"LEFT"n	&"LT"n	Turns the turtle left 'n' degrees.
&"HOME"		Moves turtle to center pointing up.
&"PENUP"	&"PU"	Raises the turtle's pen.
&"PENDOWN"	&"PD"	Lowers the turtle's pen.
&"PENCOLOR"n	&"PC"n	Sets the pen color (0-7).
&"CLEARSCREEN"	&"CS"	Clears the screen to current background color.
&"BACKGROUND"n	&"BG"n	Sets background color 'n' (0-7).
&"FULLSCREEN"	&"FS"	Sets full screen graphics mode.
&"SPLITSCREEN"	&"SS"	Sets split graphics/text mode.
&"HIDETURTLE"	&"HT"	Causes the turtle to disappear.
&"SHOWTURTLE"	&"ST"	Causes the turtle to appear on screen.
&"MOVETO"x,y	&"MT"x,y	Moves turtle to point x,y on screen.
&"TURNTO"n	&"TT"n	Turns the turtle to angle 'n'.
&"?WHERE"x,y		Sets 'x,y' to turtle's current position.
&"?COLLISION"c		Sets 'c' to zero (0) if there is no collision.
&"SING"p,d		Makes the turtle sing; 'p' = pitch, 'd' = duration.
&"PRINTOUT name"	&"PO name"	Prints program starting with defined 'name'
&"SHOWSCREEN"n		Shows screen page 'n'.
&"DRAWSCREEN"n		Sets screen for turtle to draw on.

Appendix A – Sample Programs

CIRCLES

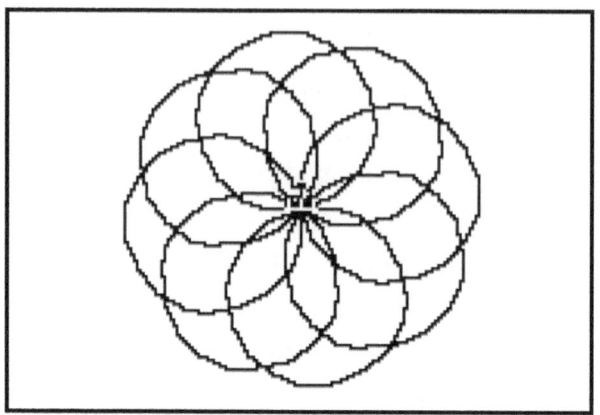

```
5   HOME : & "DRAW
7   VTAB 22: HTAB 1: CALL  -958: INPUT "WHAT ANGLE? ";ANGLE
10  & "DRAW
30  FOR I = 1 TO 360/ANGLE
40  & "CIRCLE
45  & "RIGHT "ANGLE
50  NEXT I
60  VTAB 22: CALL  -958: PRINT "PRESS A KEY TO GO ON (Q TO
    QUIT) ";: GET KEY$
65  IF KEY$ < >"Q"  THEN  GOTO 7
70  HOME : & "NODRAW
80  END
100   REM <CTRL-J>-----<CTRL-J>
101   TO "CIRCLE
110   FOR J = 1 TO 18
120   & "F "10
130   & "R "20
140   NEXT J
150   RETURN
```

GALAXY

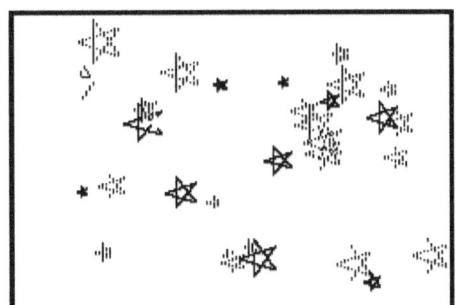

```
10  & "INITIALIZE
20  & "DRAW.UNIVERSE
30  END
100   REM <CTRL-J>-----<CTRL-J>
110   TO "DRAW.UNIVERSE
120   :: & "DECIDE.LOCATION
130   :: & "DRAW.STAR
140   :: POP : & "DRAW.UNIVERSE
200   REM <CTRL-J>-----<CTRL-J>
210   TO "DECIDE.LOCATION
220   ::X =  RND(1) *200 -100
230   ::Y =  RND(1) *140 -70
240   :: & "PENUP
250   :: & "MOVETO "X,Y
260   :: & "PENCOLOR " RND(1) *7 +1
270   :: & "PENDOWN
280   RETURN
300   REM <CTRL-J>-----<CTRL-J>
310   TO "DRAW.STAR
320   :: & "PICK.SIZE
330   :: & "STAR
340   RETURN
400   REM <CTRL-J>-----<CTRL-J>
410   TO "PICK.SIZE
420   ::SIZE =  RND(1) *20 +5
430   RETURN
500   REM <CTRL-J>-----<CTRL-J>
510   TO "STAR
520   :: FOR S = 1 TO 6
530   ::: & "FORWARD "SIZE
540   ::: & "RIGHT "144
550   :: NEXT S
560   RETURN
10000   REM <CTRL-J>-----<CTRL-J>
10010   TO "INITIALIZE
10020   :: & "DRAW
10030   :: & "FULLSCREEN
10040   RETURN
```

GRUB

```
10   & "INIT.FIELD
20   & "PERAMBULATE.TURTLE
30   GOTO 10
100   REM <CTRL-J>-----<CTRL-J>
110   TO "INIT.FIELD
115   :: HOME : & "DRAW
120   :: & "PENUP
125   :: & "MOVETO " -130, -90
130   :: & "PENDOWN
135   :: & "FULLSCREEN
140   :: FOR S = 1 TO 2: & "DRAW.HALF.SQUARE": NEXT S
145   :: FOR L = 1 TO 15: & "DRAW.RANDOM.LINE": NEXT L
150   :: & "PENUP
155   :: & "HOME
157   RETURN
160   REM <CTRL-J>-----<CTRL-J>
165   TO "DRAW.HALF.SQUARE
170   :: & "FD "180: & "RT "90
175   :: & "FD "260: & "RT "90
180   RETURN
200   REM <CTRL-J>-----<CTRL-J>
210   TO "DRAW.RANDOM.LINE
215   ::CH =  RND(1)
220   :: IF CH <.5  THEN  & "DRAW.VERTICAL.LINE
225   :: IF CH < = .5  THEN  & "DRAW.HORIZONTAL.LINE
230   RETURN
240   REM <CTRL-J>-----<CTRL-J>
250   TO "DRAW.VERTICAL.LINE
255   :: & "PICK.POINTS
260   :: & "PU": & "MT"P1,P2: & "PD": & "MT"P1,P3: RETURN
265   RETURN
266   REM <CTRL-J>-----<CTRL-J>
270   TO "DRAW.HORIZONTAL.LINE
275   :: & "PICK.POINTS
280   :: & "PU": & "MT"P1,P3: & "PD": & "MT"P2,P3: RETURN
285   REM <CTRL-J>-----<CTRL-J>
290   TO "PICK.POINTS
295   ::P1 =  RND(1) *178 -89:P2 =  RND(1) *178 -89:P3 =
      RND(1) *178 -89: RETURN
300   REM <CTRL-J>-----<CTRL-J>
310   TO "PERAMBULATE.TURTLE
315   : FOR M = 1 TO 250
320   :: & "FORWARD "2: IF  RND(1) <.1  THEN  & "SING"1,5
325   :: & "?COLLISION "C
330   :: IF C < >0  THEN  & "TT" RND(1) *360
340   : NEXT M
350   RETURN
```

BERSERK SINGING TURTLE

```
10   & "DRAW
15   & "FULLSCREEN
30   FOR I = 1 TO 80
40   X =  RND(1) *278 -139
50   Y =  RND(1) *190 -95
60   C =  RND(1) *8
65   P =  RND(1) *256
70   & "PENCOLOR "C
80   & "MOVETO "X,Y
85   & "SING "P,3
90   NEXT I
92   & "BACKGROUND " RND(1) *8
93   FOR W = 1 TO 1000: NEXT W
95   & "CLEARSCREEN
100   GOTO 30
```

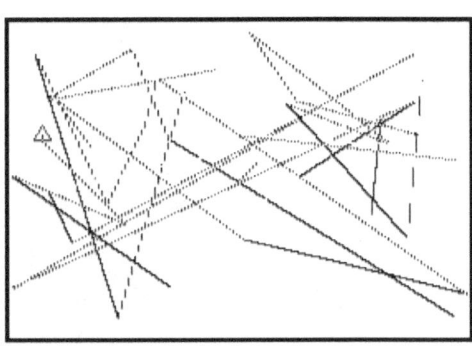

SUNBURST TURTLE

```
10   & "DRAW
20   & "HIDETURTLE
30   & "FULLSCREEN
35   REM <CTRL-J>-----<CTRL-J>
40   & "HOME
50   & "TURNTO     " RND(1) *360
60   & "PENCOLOR   " RND(1) *7
70   & "FORWARD    " RND(1) *90
80   GOTO 40
```

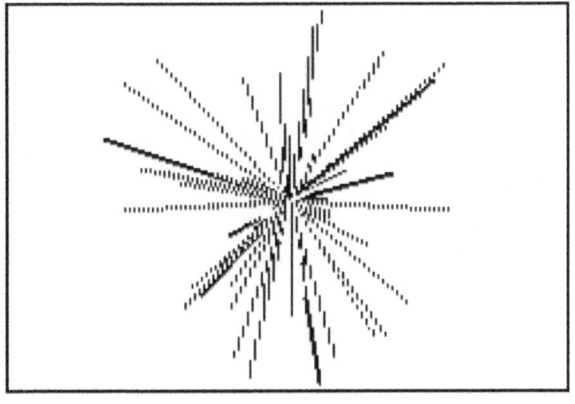

SPIRAL SQUARE

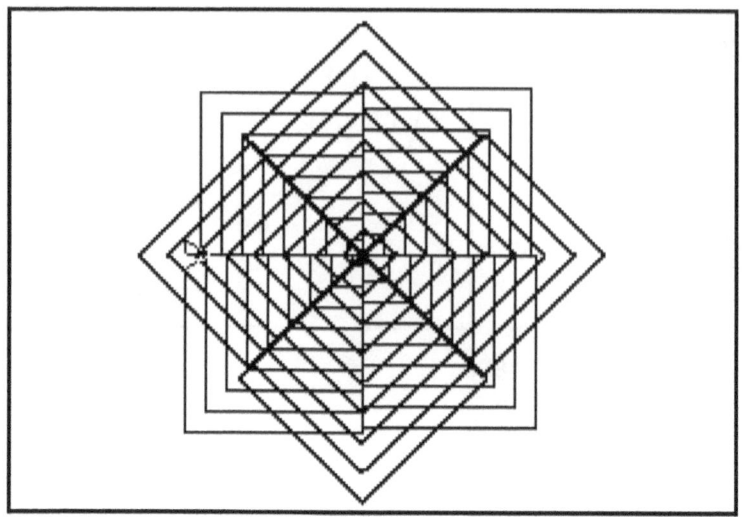

```
5   ONERR  GOTO 200
10  & "NODRAW": HOME : VTAB 23: INPUT "WHAT ANGLE? ";ANG
15  REM <CTRL-J>-----<CTRL-J>
20  & "DRAW
30  & "FULLSCREEN
35  SIDE = 0: & "SPIRAL
39  REM <CTRL-J>-----<CTRL-J>
40  TO "SPIRAL ;SIDE,ANG
45  & "SQUARE
50  & "RIGHT "ANG
55  SIDE = SIDE +1
60  POP : & "SPIRAL
100  REM <CTRL-J>-----<CTRL-J>
101  TO "SQUARE
110  FOR I = 1 TO 4
120  & "FORWARD "SIDE
130  & "RIGHT "90
140  NEXT I
150  RETURN
200  REM <CTRL-J>-----<CTRL-J>
202  IF  PEEK(222) = 255  THEN 230
205  & "SPLITSCREEN
210  HOME : VTAB 23: PRINT "PRESS A KEY TO GO ON (Q TO
     QUIT)";: GET KEY$
220  IF KEY$ < >"Q"  THEN 10
230  HOME : & "NODRAW
240  END
```

QUICK CONFUSION

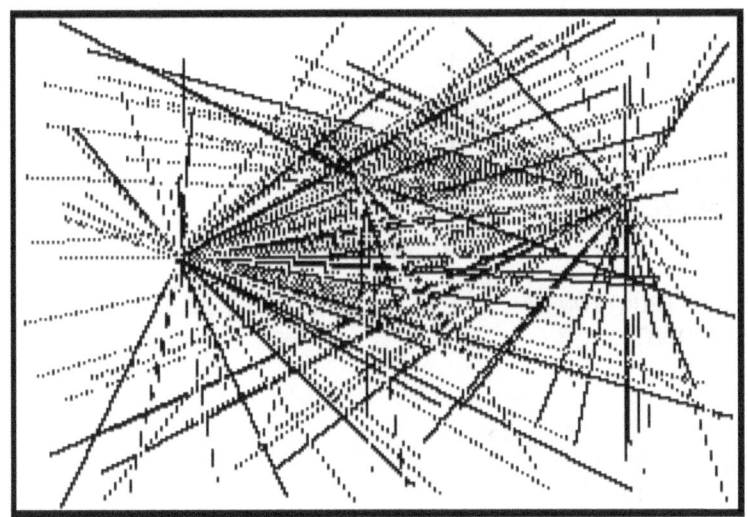

```
10    & "DRAW
15    & "FULLSCREEN
20    & "BACKGROUND "3
35    & "HIDETURTLE
37    REM <CTRL-J>-----<CTRL-J>
40    & "PICK.X.AND.Y
50    X = XP:Y = YP
60    & "SUNBURST
70    GOTO 40
100   REM <CTRL-J>-----<CTRL-J>
101   TO "SUNBURST
105   FOR SB = 1 TO 100
110   :: & "PENUP
120   :: & "MOVETO    "X,Y
130   :: & "PENDOWN
140   :: & "PENCOLOR " RND(1) *7
150   :: & "PICK.X.AND.Y
160   :: & "MOVETO    "XP,YP
170   NEXT SB
180   RETURN
200   REM <CTRL-J>-----<CTRL-J>
201   TO "PICK.X.AND.Y
210   XP =  RND(1) *278 -139
220   YP =  RND(1) *190 -95
230   RETURN
```

INSTANT TURTLE

```
10   ONERR GOTO 30
20   & "INITIALIZE
30   & "GETINSTRUCTION
40   & "DOINSTRUCTION
50   GOTO 30
90   REM <CTRL-J>-----<CTRL-J>
100  TO "INITIALIZE
105  & "DRAW
110  HOME
115  & "WRITE.INSTRUCTIONS
120  & "WRITE.PROMPT
125  STP = 3:BG = 0
130  RETURN
200  REM <CTRL-J>-----<CTRL-J>
210  TO "GETINSTRUCTION
220  VTAB 21: HTAB 14
230  GET IN$
240  RETURN
300  REM <CTRL-J>-----<CTRL-J>
310  TO "DOINSTRUCTION
320  IF IN$ = "K"  THEN  & "FORWARD "STP
340  IF IN$ = "J"  THEN  & "LEFT "30
350  IF IN$ = "L"  THEN  & "RIGHT "30
360  IF IN$ = "D"  THEN  & "PENDOWN
365  IF IN$ = "U"  THEN  & "PENUP
370  IF IN$ = "C"  THEN  & "INITIALIZE
380  IF IN$ = "B"  THEN  & "CHANGE.BACKGROUND
381  IF IN$ = "S"  THEN  & "SAVE.PICTURE
382  IF IN$ = "R"  THEN  & "READ.PICTURE
385  IF ASC(IN$) = 13 THEN  & "SHOW.INSTRUCTIONS
390  RETURN
400  REM <CTRL-J>-----<CTRL-J>
401  TO "CHANGE.BACKGROUND
410  BG = BG +1: IF BG >7  THEN BG = 0
420  & "BACKGROUND "BG
430  RETURN
500  REM <CTRL-J>-----<CTRL-J>
505  TO "WRITE.INSTRUCTIONS
510  VTAB 1: HTAB 13: INVERSE : PRINT "- INSTRUCTIONS -":
     NORMAL : PRINT
515  ST$ = "K - MOVES THE TURTLE FORWARD": & "WRITE.INSTRUCTION.LINE
520  ST$ = "J - TURNS THE TURTLE LEFT": & "WRITE.INSTRUCTION.LINE
525  ST$ = "L - TURNS THE TURTLE RIGHT": & "WRITE.INSTRUCTION.LINE
530  ST$ = "D - PUTS THE PEN DOWN": & "WRITE.INSTRUCTION.LINE
535  ST$ = "U - TAKES THE PEN UP": & "WRITE.INSTRUCTION.LINE
```

```
550   ST$ = "C - CLEARS THE SCREEN": & "WRITE.INSTRUCTION.LINE
555   ST$ = "B - CHANGES THE BACKGROUND": & "WRITE.INSTRUCTION.LINE
560   ST$ = "S - SAVES A PICTURE ON DISK": & "WRITE.INSTRUCTION.LINE
570   ST$ = "R - READS A PICTURE ON DISK": & "WRITE.INSTRUCTION.LINE
580   RETURN
600   REM <CTRL-J>-----<CTRL-J>
601   TO "SHOW.INSTRUCTIONS
605   & "NODRAW
610   HTAB 1: VTAB 21: CALL  -958
615   VTAB 24: PRINT "PRESS <RETURN> TO GO BACK TO PICTURE.";
620   GET IN$: IF  ASC(IN$) < >13  THEN 620
625   HTAB 1: VTAB 21: CALL  -958: & "WRITE.PROMPT
630   & "SHOWSCREEN "1
635   RETURN
700   REM <CTRL-J>-----<CTRL-J>
705   TO "WRITE.PROMPT
710   VTAB 24: PRINT "PRESS <RETURN> TO SEE CHOICES";: VTAB 21:
      HTAB 1: INVERSE : PRINT "INSTRUCTION?";: NORMAL
720   RETURN
800   REM <CTRL-J>-----<CTRL-J>
801   TO "SAVE.PICTURE
802   ONERR  GOTO 1310
805   HOME : & "NODRAW
810   VTAB 8: INPUT "USING WHAT NAME? ";NAME$
811   IF NAME$ = ""  THEN 828
815   & "SHOWSCREEN "1
816   HOME : VTAB 23: PRINT "SAVING PICTURE "NAME$"..."
817   & "HIDETURTLE
818   & "SAVE.STATE
820   PRINT  CHR$(4)"BSAVE PICTURE."NAME$",A$2000,L$1FFF"
825   & "RESTORE.STATE
826   & "SHOWTURTLE
828   & "SHOWSCREEN "1
830   HOME
835   & "WRITE.INSTRUCTIONS
840   & "WRITE.PROMPT
845   ONERR  GOTO 30
850   RETURN
900   REM <CTRL-J>-----<CTRL-J>
901   TO "READ.PICTURE
902   ONERR  GOTO 1310
905   HOME : & "NODRAW
910   VTAB 8: INPUT "WHAT PICTURE NAME? ";NAME$
915   IF NAME$ = ""  THEN 942
916   & "DRAW
920   & "HIDETURTLE
925   & "SAVE.STATE
930   PRINT  CHR$(4)"BLOAD PICTURE."NAME$
935   & "RESTORE.STATE
```

```
940   & "SHOWTURTLE
942   & "SHOWSCREEN "1
945   HOME : & "WRITE.INSTRUCTIONS
950   & "WRITE.PROMPT
955   ONERR  GOTO 30
960   RETURN
1000  REM <CTRL-J>-----<CTRL-J>
1001  TO "SAVE.STATE
1005  :: & "?WHERE "XS,YS
1010  :: & "?DIR    "DIR
1015  RETURN
1100  REM <CTRL-J>-----<CTRL-J>
1105  TO "RESTORE.STATE
1110  :: & "DRAWSCREEN "1
1115  :: & "PENUP
1120  :: & "HOME
1125  :: & "MOVETO "XS,YS
1130  :: & "TURNTO "DIR
1135  :: & "PENDOWN
1140  RETURN
1200  REM <CTRL-J>-----<CTRL-J>
1201  TO "WRITE.INSTRUCTION.LINE
1205  PRINT : HTAB 7: PRINT  LEFT$(ST$,1);: NORMAL
1210  PRINT  RIGHT$(ST$, LEN(ST$) -1)
1220  RETURN
1300  REM <CTRL-J>-----<CTRL-J>
1305  TO "PROCESS.ERROR
1310  ERR =  PEEK(222)
1320  IF ERR < >9  THEN 1350
1325  : HOME : VTAB 23: PRINT "DISK FULL...": FOR W = 1
      TO 700: NEXT W
1330  & "RESTORE.STATE
1335  & "SHOWTURTLE
1340  & "SHOWSCREEN "1
1345  GOTO 1390
1350  IF ERR < >6  THEN 1380
1355  : HOME : VTAB 23: PRINT NAME$" NOT FOUND...": FOR W = 1
      TO 700: NEXT W
1360  GOTO 1330
1365  GOTO 1390
1380  : HOME : VTAB 23: PRINT "ERROR...": FOR W = 1 TO 700:
      NEXT W
1385  GOTO 1330
1390  ONERR  GOTO 30
1391  HOME
1392  & "WRITE.INSTRUCTIONS
1393  & "WRITE.PROMPT
1395  GOTO 30
```

DYNATRACK

```
4    & "INTRODUCTION
5    & "DYNATURTLE
6    END
9    REM -----------------
10   TO "DYNATURTLE
20   :: & "INIT.DYNA
30   :: & "DO.DYNA.TURTLE
40   RETURN
99   REM -----------------
100  TO "INIT.DYNA
110  :: & "DRAW
115  :: & "FULLSCREEN
116  :: & "INIT.TRACK
125  :: & "INIT.POSITION
160  RETURN
199  REM -----------------------
200  TO "DO.DYNA.TURTLE
210  :: & "MOVE.TURTLE
220  :: & "COMMAND
230  :: IF (FIN)  THEN  & "QUIT
240  :: & "CHECK.COLLISION
250  GOTO 210
299  REM -----------------------
300  TO "MOVE.TURTLE
310  ::X1 = X +VX
315  :: IF  ABS(X1) >138  THEN X1 = X:VX = 0
316  ::X = X1
320  ::Y1 = Y +VY
325  :: IF  ABS(Y1) >94  THEN Y1 = Y:VY = 0
326  ::Y = Y1
330  :: & "MOVETO "X,Y
340  RETURN
399  REM -----------------------
400  TO "COMMAND
410  :: & "READKEY
420  :: IF KEY$ = "J"  THEN  & "DYNALEFT
430  :: IF KEY$ = "L"  THEN  & "DYNARIGHT
440  :: IF KEY$ = "K"  THEN  & "DYNAKICK
450  :: IF KEY$ = "Q"  THEN FIN = 1: RETURN
460  RETURN
499  REM -----------------------
500  TO "READKEY
510  KEY$ = ""
520  :: IF  PEEK( -16384) <128  THEN  RETURN
530  :: GET KEY$
540  RETURN
```

```
             DYNATRACK
THIS PROGRAM SHOWS HOW YOU CAN USE THE
TURTLE FOR SOME SIMPLE ANIMATION.

TO USE THE PROGRAM TRY TO KEEP THE
THE TURTLE IN THE TRACK BETWEEN THE
TWO CIRCLES.

     K - KICKS THE TURTLE FORWARD
     J - TURNS THE TURTLE LEFT
     L - TURNS THE TURTLE RIGHT
     Q - QUITS

          PRESS A KEY TO BEGIN
```

```
599    REM ----------------------
600    TO "DYNALEFT
605    :: & "LEFT "30
610    :: & "?DIRECTION "D
620    ::D = D *A2R
630    RETURN
699    REM ----------------------
700    TO "DYNARIGHT
705    :: & "RIGHT "30
710    :: & "?DIRECTION "D
720    ::D = D *A2R
730    RETURN
799    REM ----------------------
800    TO "DYNAKICK
810    ::VX = VX + COS(D)
820    ::VY = VY + SIN(D)
830    RETURN
899    REM ----------------------
900    TO "INIT.TRACK
910    ::SIDE = 2: & "CCIRCLE
920    ::SIDE = 4: & "CCIRCLE
960    RETURN
999    REM ----------------------
1000   TO "CCIRCLE
1010   :: & "PENUP
1020   & "MOVETO " -60 *SIDE/3.142,0
1025   :: & "PENDOWN
1030   :: FOR I = 1 TO 120
1040   ::: & "FORWARD "SIDE
1050   ::: & "RIGHT "3
1060   :: NEXT I
1095   RETURN
1099   REM ----------------------
1110   TO "QUIT
1120   HOME : & "NODRAW
1130   END
1200   REM ----------------------
1205   TO "CHECK.COLLISION
1210   :: & "?COLLISION "CL: IF CL = 0  THEN  RETURN
1215   :: & "MAKE.GROSS.NOISE
1220   :: & "INIT.POSITION"
1245   RETURN
1300   REM ----------------------
1305   TO "INIT.POSITION
1306   & "PENUP
1310   ::VX = 0:VY = 0
1320   ::A2R = 3.14159/180
```

```
1325  :: & "MOVETO " -180/3.142,0: & "TURNTO "90
1330  :: & "?WHERE "X,Y
1340  :: & "?DIRECTION "D
1350  ::D = D *A2R
1360  ::FIN = 0
1370  RETURN
1400  REM ----------------------
1410  TO "MAKE.GROSS.NOISE
1420  :: FOR SD = 1 TO 50:S2 =  PEEK( -16336): NEXT SD
1430  RETURN
1999  REM ----------------------
2000  TO "INTRODUCTION
2010  & "ND": HOME
2020  INVERSE : HTAB 16: PRINT "DYNATRACK": NORMAL
2030  PRINT : PRINT "THIS PROGRAM SHOWS HOW YOU CAN USE THE"
2040  PRINT : PRINT "TURTLE FOR SOME SIMPLE ANIMATION."
2050  PRINT : PRINT : PRINT "TO USE THE PROGRAM TRY TO KEEP THE"
2060  PRINT : PRINT "THE TURTLE IN THE TRACK BETWEEN THE"
2070  PRINT : PRINT "TWO CIRCLES."
2080  PRINT : PRINT : PRINT "     K - KICKS THE TURTLE FORWARD"
2090  PRINT : PRINT "     J - TURNS THE TURTLE LEFT"
2100  PRINT : PRINT "     L - TURNS THE TURTLE RIGHT"
2110  PRINT : PRINT "     Q - QUITS"
2115  INVERSE
2120  VTAB 24: HTAB 11: PRINT "PRESS A KEY TO BEGIN";
2125  NORMAL
2130  POKE  -16368,0
2150  GET A$: HOME : RETURN
```

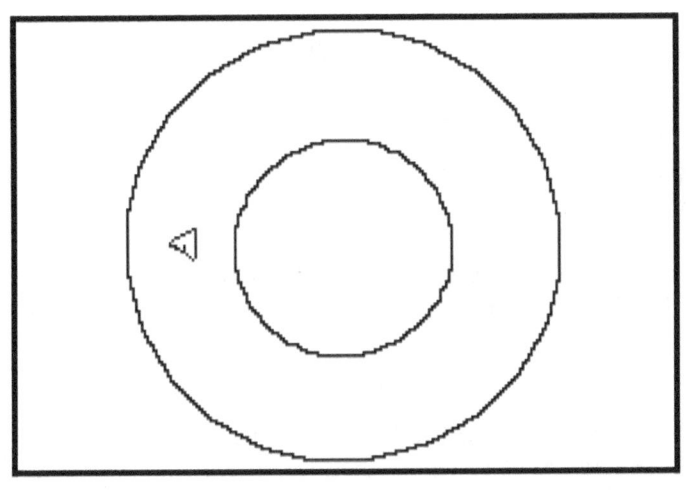

SIERPINSKI

```
5   REM  *** MAIN PROGRAM ***
6   :
10  & "INTRODUCTION
20  & "INPUT.PARAMETERS
30  & "SET.UP.START
40  & "SIERPINSKI
45  & "HIDETURTLE
50  & "CHECK.KEYPRESS
60  GOTO 20
499  REM <CTRL-J>*** DRAW SIERPINSKI CV.<CTRL-J>
500  TO "SIERPINSKI ;SIDE LEVEL
510  : FOR I = 1 TO 4
515  ::LEVEL = L1
520  :: & "ONESIDE
530  :: & "RT "45
540  :: & "FD "SIDE/ SQR(2)
550  :: & "RT "45
555  : NEXT I
560  : RETURN
599  REM <CTRL-J>*** DO ONE SIDE OF CV.<CTRL-J>
600  TO "ONESIDE ;SIDE LEVEL
610  : IF LEVEL < = 0  THEN LEVEL = LEVEL +1: RETURN
620  :LEVEL = LEVEL -1: & "ONESIDE
630  : & "RT "45
640  : & "FD "SIDE/ SQR(2)
650  : & "RT "45
660  :LEVEL = LEVEL -1: & "ONESIDE
662  : & "LT "90
665  : & "FD "SIDE
667  : & "LT "90
670  :LEVEL = LEVEL -1: & "ONESIDE
680  : & "RT "45
690  : & "FD "SIDE/ SQR(2)
700  : & "RT "45
710  :LEVEL = LEVEL -1: & "ONESIDE
715  :LEVEL = LEVEL +1
720  RETURN
4999  REM <CTRL-J>*** CHECK KEYPRESS<CTRL-J>
5000  TO "CHECK.KEYPRESS
5010  POKE  -16368,0
5020  GET A$
5030  RETURN
6999  REM <CTRL-J>*** SET UP START<CTRL-J>
7000  TO "SET.UP.START
7010  HOME : & "DRAW
7020  & "PENUP
```

```
7025  P = SIDE/2
7030  & "MOVETO " -60, -60 +P
7040  & "BACKGROUND "3
7050  & "PENCOLOR   "0
7060  & "PENDOWN
7070  & "FULLSCREEN
7080  RETURN
7999  REM <CTRL-J>*** INPUT PARAMETERS<CTRL-J>
8000  TO "INPUT.PARAMETERS
8005  & "NODRAW
8010  HOME : VTAB 7
8015  NORMAL
8020  PRINT "TYPE IN THE NUMBER OF LEVELS TO GO TO"
8030  PRINT : PRINT "IN DRAWING THE CURVE.  THE GREATER THE"
8040  PRINT : PRINT "NUMBER OF LEVELS THE MORE COMPLEX THE"
8050  PRINT : PRINT "CURVE WILL BE."
8060  PRINT : PRINT : INVERSE : PRINT "NUMBER OF LEVELS (1-6)? "
      ;: GET LV$
8070  L1 = VAL(LV$): IF L1 <1  OR L1 >6  THEN  PRINT  CHR$(7);:
      GOTO 8010
8075  REM <CTRL-J>... CENTER FIGURE BY
8076  REM     SETTING SIDE LENGTH<CTRL-J>
8080  ND = 2 ^L1 -1
8090  N1 = 120 * SQR(2)
8100  N2 = (2 *ND +2)/ SQR(2) +ND * SQR(2)
8110  SIDE = N1/N2
8120  RETURN
8999  REM <CTRL-J>*** GO ON BY KEY-PRESS<CTRL-J>
9000  TO "GO.ON
9010  VTAB 24: HTAB 9: PRINT "PRESS A KEY TO CONTINUE";
9020  GET A$: RETURN
9999  REM <CTRL-J>*** INTRODUCTION<CTRL-J>
10000  TO "INTRODUCTION
10005  NORMAL
10010  HOME : & "ND
10020  VTAB 5: PRINT "THIS PROGRAM DRAWS A SPACE FILLING"
10030  VTAB 7: PRINT "CURVE CALLED A SIERPINSKI CURVE."
10040  VTAB 9: PRINT "IT USES A RECURSIVE DEFINITION."
10050  & "GO.ON
10060  RETURN
```

WINDOWS

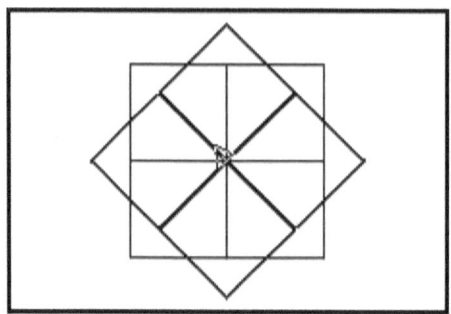

```
5     & "DRAW
10    HOME : VTAB 23: INPUT "WHAT ANGLE? ";ANGLE
20    & "DRAW
30    & "FULLSCREEN
40    & "TWIRL
45    & "SPLITSCREEN
50    HOME : VTAB 23: PRINT "PRESS A KEY TO GO ON (Q TO QUIT)";:
      GET KEY$
60    IF KEY$ < >"Q"  THEN 10
70    HOME : & "NODRAW
80    END
1000  REM <CTRL-J>-----<CTRL-J>
1001  TO "SQUARE
1010  & "FORWARD "50
1020  & "RIGHT "90
1030  & "FORWARD "50
1040  & "RIGHT "90
1050  & "FORWARD "50
1060  & "RIGHT "90
1070  & "FORWARD "50
1080  RETURN
2000  REM <CTRL-J>-----<CTRL-J>
2001  TO "WINDOW
2010  & "SQUARE
2020  & "SQUARE
2030  & "SQUARE
2040  & "SQUARE
2050  RETURN
3000  REM <CTRL-J>-----<CTRL-J>
3001  TO "TWIRL
3010  FOR I = 1 TO 20
3020  & "WINDOW
3030  & "RIGHT "ANGLE
3040  NEXT I
3050  RETURN
```

POLYSTOP

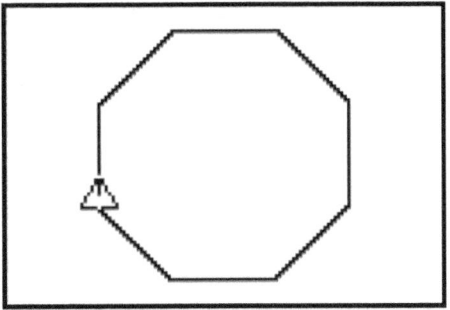

```
5   HOME
10  & "DRAW
20  & "GET.INPUT
30  & "POLYSTOP
40  & "WAIT.KEYPRESS
50  IF KEY$ = "Q"  THEN  & "QUIT
60  GOTO 20
99  REM <CTRL-J>-----<CTRL-J>
100  TO "GET.INPUT
105  :: HOME
110  :: VTAB 22
120  :: INPUT "WHAT ANGLE ? ";ANG
130  :: INPUT "SIDE LENGTH? ";SIDE
140  :: & "CLEARSCREEN
160  RETURN
199  REM <CTRL-J>-----<CTRL-J>
200  TO "POLYSTOP
210  ::TURN = 0
215  :: IF TURN >0  AND TURN - INT(TURN/360) *360 = 0 THEN
     RETURN
220  :: & "FORWARD "SIDE
230  :: & "RIGHT    "ANG
250  ::TURN = TURN +ANG
260  :: GOTO 215
299  REM <CTRL-J>-----<CTRL-J>
300  TO "WAIT.KEYPRESS
305  HOME : VTAB 23: PRINT "PRESS A KEY TO GO ON (Q TO QUIT)";:
     GET KEY$
330  RETURN
399  REM <CTRL-J>-----<CTRL-J>
400  TO "QUIT
410  HOME : & "NODRAW
420  END
```

SNOWFLAKE

```
5    & "INTRODUCTION
10   & "INPUT.PARAMETERS
20   & "SET.UP.START
30   & "SNOWFLAKE
35   & "WAIT.KEYPRESS
40   GOTO 5
100  REM <CTRL-J>-----<CTRL-J>
101  TO "SNOWFLAKE   ;LEVEL SIDE
110  : FOR I = 1 TO 3
120  :: & "FACE
130  :: & "RIGHT "120
140  : NEXT I
150  RETURN
200  REM <CTRL-J>-----<CTRL-J>
201  TO "FACE    ;LEVEL SIDE
210  :LEVEL = LEVEL -1
220  : IF LEVEL > = 0  THEN  GOTO 260
230  :: & "FORWARD "SIDE
240  ::LEVEL = LEVEL +1
250  :: RETURN
260  : & "FACE
270  : & "LEFT "60
280  : & "FACE
290  : & "RIGHT "120
300  : & "FACE
310  : & "LEFT "60
320  : & "FACE
330  :LEVEL = LEVEL +1
340  RETURN
400  REM <CTRL-J>-----<CTRL-J>
401  TO "INPUT.PARAMETERS
410  INVERSE : VTAB 19: HTAB 1: PRINT "LEVELS? (1-5) ";: GET
     LEVEL$: NORMAL :LEVEL = VAL(LEVEL$)
420  IF LEVEL <1  OR LEVEL >5  THEN  PRINT  CHR$(7);: GOTO 410
430  SIDE = 180/(2 * SQR(3) *3 ^(LEVEL -1))
440  NORMAL
470  HOME : RETURN
500  REM <CTRL-J>-----<CTRL-J>
501  TO "SET.UP.START
510  & "DRAW
520  & "RIGHT "30
540  & "PENUP
550  & "MOVETO " -45 * SQR(3), -45
560  & "PENDOWN
570  & "FULLSCREEN
580  RETURN
```

```
600  REM <CTRL-J>-----<CTRL-J>
601  TO "INTRODUCTION
602  & "NODRAW
604  HOME : INVERSE : HTAB 13: PRINT "SNOWFLAKE CURVE": NORMAL
605  PRINT : PRINT : PRINT "THIS PROGRAM DRAWS WHAT IS CALLED A"
610  PRINT : PRINT "SNOWFLAKE CURVE.  IT IS A RECURSIVELY"
615  PRINT : PRINT "DEFINED CURVE.  AT EACH LEVEL THE"
620  PRINT : PRINT "CURVE BECOMES MORE COMPLEX."
625  PRINT : PRINT : PRINT "AFTER THE CURVE IS DRAWN, PRESS A
     KEY"
630  PRINT : PRINT "TO TRY ANOTHER ONE."
640  RETURN
700  REM <CTRL-J>-----<CTRL-J>
701  TO "WAIT.KEYPRESS
710  : & "HIDETURTLE
720  POKE  -16368,0
730  : GET KEY$
750  : & "SHOWTURTLE
760  RETURN
```

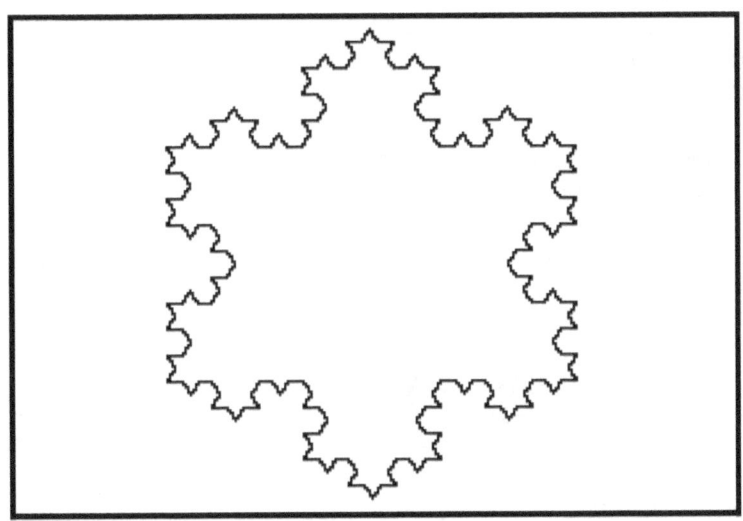

SPIRAL

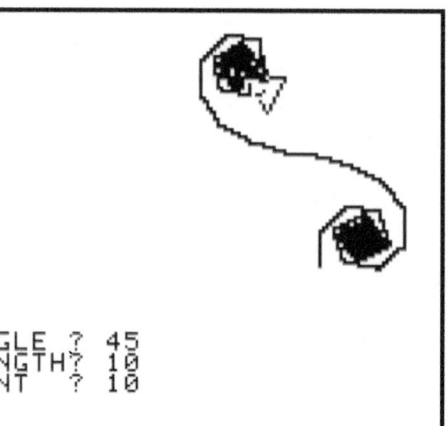

```
WHAT ANGLE ? 45
SIDE LENGTH? 10
INCREMENT  ? 10
```

```
5   HOME
10  & "DRAW
20  & "GET.INPUT
30  & "SPIRAL
99  REM <CTRL-J>-----<CTRL-J>
100  TO "GET.INPUT
105  HOME
110  :: VTAB 22
120  :: INPUT "WHAT ANGLE ? ";ANG
130  :: INPUT "SIDE LENGTH? ";SIDE
135  :: INPUT "INCREMENT  ? ";INC
140  :: & "CLEARSCREEN
160  RETURN
199  REM <CTRL-J>-----<CTRL-J>
200  TO "SPIRAL
210  & "MOVE.FORWARD.AND.TURN
230  ::ANGLE = ANGLE +INC
240  :: GOTO 210
250  RETURN
399  REM <CTRL-J>-----<CTRL-J>
400  TO "MOVE.FORWARD.AND.TURN
410  :: & "FORWARD "SIDE
420  :: & "RIGHT   "ANGLE
430  RETURN
```

FIGURE EIGHT

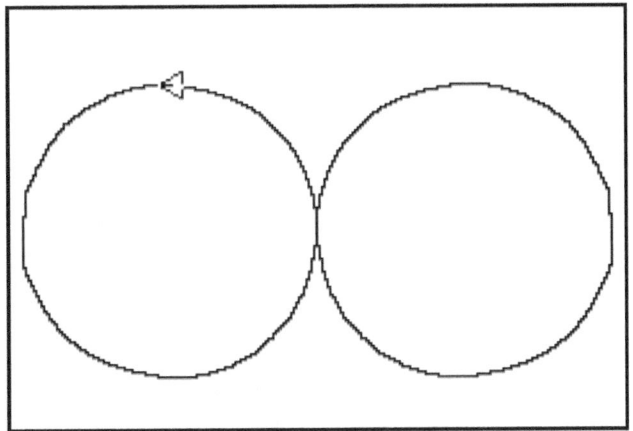

```
10   & "DRAW
20   & "FULLSCREEN
30   & "PENDOWN
40   & "CIRCLE.RIGHT
50   & "CIRCLE.LEFT
60   GOTO 40
99   REM ------------------------
100   TO "CIRCLE.RIGHT
110   FOR I = 1 TO 36
120   & "RIGHT    "10
130   & "FORWARD "10
140   NEXT I
150   RETURN
199   REM ------------------------
200   TO "CIRCLE.LEFT
210   FOR I = 1 TO 36
220   & "LEFT     "10
230   & "FORWARD "10
240   NEXT I
250   RETURN
```

www.ingramcontent.com/pod-product-compliance
Lightning Source LLC
Chambersburg PA
CBHW021940170526
45157CB00005B/2362